HEMISPHERE

HEMISPHERE

POEMS

Ellen Hagan

For Sonia —
Because you dial thought
if you. Rise up, always!

TRIQUARTERLY BOOKS
NORTHWESTERN UNIVERSITY PRESS
EVANSTON, ILLINOIS

TriQuarterly Books
Northwestern University Press
www.nupress.northwestern.edu

Copyright © 2015 by Ellen Hagan. Published 2015 by TriQuarterly Books / Northwestern University Press. All rights reserved.

Printed in the United States of America

10   9   8   7   6   5   4   3   2

Library of Congress Cataloging-in-Publication Data
Hagan, Ellen, author.
    Hemisphere : poems / Ellen Hagan.
      pages cm
    Includes bibliographical references.
    ISBN 978-0-8101-3080-7 (pbk. : alk. paper)
    I. Title.
    PS3608.A338H46 2015
    811.6—dc23
                                       2014037056

Contents

◗

III. Conception/Concept

Acknowledgments

For the collective families of the following: Bazaz, Dawson, Flores, Hagan, and Sferra.

For the family collectives of the following: Affrilachian Poets, Bardstown, Conjwoman, DreamYard, girlstory, GlobalWrites, Governor's School for the Arts, Kentucky, Northern Manhattan Arts Alliance, Northwestern University Press (Anne Gendler for her pristine editorial vision and Marianne Jankowski for her rainbow cover brilliance), NYC, Sawyer House Press, and VONA.

For Parneshia Jones and her supreme vision and hunger and genius and journey.

For Lisa Ascalon, Dan Bernitt, Megan Clark-Garriga, Ama Codjoe, Mitchell L. H. Douglas, Dana Edell, Kelly Norman Ellis, Lisa Forsee-Roby, Tanya Gallo, Aracelis Girmay, Nanya-Akuki Goodrich, Andrée Greene, Lindsey Homra-Siroky, Melissa Johnson, Caroline Kennedy, Rob Linné, Kamilah Aisha Moon, Carrie Nath, Willie Perdomo, Zahida Pirani, Danni Quintos, Carla Repice, Naomi Shihab-Nye, Renée Watson, Kelly Wheatley, and Marina Wilson, for your many poet and artist eyes and your willingness to friend and drink and dance and ride through this life alongside me.

And for David—what sweet and balm and bless and calm and love you continue to bring—oh, thank you and love.

Especially and always for: Araceli and Miriam—for the daughters, dragons, kites, and oceans you two are.

❯

To the editors of the following journals and anthologies—thank you.

Blood Lotus: "Holy, Holy" and "Words You Say"

Huizache: "The Hunt" and "Ones Heading Home" ("Oncoming")

Jelly Bucket: "Celi Visits American Museum of Natural History," "Foot or Fist," "Mercy," and "24 weeks—16 to go"

PLUCK! The Journal of Affrilachian Arts and Culture: "Notes from Aziz Bazaz," "Puberty," "Revolve," and "What It Takes"

Tidal Basin Review: "Water Sign"

"Kentucky—You Be" and "Mint Julep" appeared in *Small Batch* (Georgetown, Two of Cups Press, 2013).

HEMISPHERE

I. NAMING

LESSONS ON SPELLING

Bring the snakes in their skins, sly
& surrender. Simple bodies of grass
& clover, their slithering & sleuth-ness.
& the earth & the dusty fishermen
in from their boats, bobbing. Bring
piano, bring pain. That yellow skirt
pocked w/ fuchsia & the halter
of your mother's pixie '60s ways.
Let out the hems from your dresses,
the vertebrae in your back, body
forget skeleton—be loose, let it be dirty.
Get there. Call the black cat promenade,
lazy through the streets. Let your hair
down. Let it crawl, crowd the length
of your back. Bring soca & fiddle,
that record player your father bought
your mother in 1974. Bring all the days
from 1974 & on because time is a revolver.
A bag of limes on your back porch
squeezed & bitter & neon & orbiting
over you. Is your neighbor calling.
Is satsumas bursting on your tongue.
Bring your shiny shoes & arched soles
for the flapping pageant of second line
parade, the 100 parades from now until.
Autumnal. Hymns. Prayers.
Ways to say yes. Bring w/ you
your rope of hide, your many rings
of muscle & the washcloth
for your stomach, your feet

for the laying nape of your neck.
Bring danger & ways to hold your lips,
your lips, bring them too.
Spanning the whole of you.
You become.

WHAT IT TAKES

for my grandfather—Aziz Bazaz

Carrier of names, the 100
names carving. Carved to you.
Aziz changed to Albert.
American-ized. Simplified. Un-
dressed of culture. Ethnic
cleansed for Western tongues.
Aziz to Albert. Razook to Roscoe.

Call me by my name. I want
to say. *Say.* Un-tie the trillion tongues
the languages coiled. Un-leash
un-comfortable pronunciations.
Pronounce the letters slow.

Be what it means to carry
my name.

TO BE ALONE

We take the 11C bus at the George Washington Bus Terminal to Park Ridge, New Jersey. We go for breakfast with your great-grandmother, Elinor Sferra Bazaz, and your grandmother—my mother (your Nina)—Gianina Lynne Bazaz Hagan. And you, little girl, will be Araceli Hagan Flores when you are born. Oh little girl of many, many names, all of them yours. And of course, I am your mother. Already, I don't want you to forget that, don't want you to forget the kind of women you are born from. I want you to know who you are, want you to know all you are capable of too.

It is one of those mornings that stays. New Jersey can sometimes feel like the country. In your great-grandmother's yard, she has planted "Knockout" roses, their small, sleek bodies rising out of the soil, black-eyed Susans, phlox and bee balm, and others too, but phlox and bee balm I remember, and love, and think you are already a phlox/flock inside me, already balm, already black-eyed and lush. I want to know how to garden one day, want to be able to teach it to you. I want to know how to plant something and watch it grow into a row of other things.

Great-Grandma, who wants to be called Grandma Bazaz, is ninety-two. She is glamorous, with white hair and subtle pink lipstick, with clean, white Keds and a gold necklace with a pair of lips hanging around her still delicate neck. She still has got it. This is certain. Your great-grandfather, her husband: Albert (Aziz) Bazaz, passed away nearly fifteen years ago, and it is Grandma Bazaz who has been holding her home and family down since then. It is her garden, to tend all by herself, and *look*, I want to say to you, my unborn daughter, *look what your women are capable of. Look at what you can do. Look at all you can grow. Keep watching. Keep listening.*

We sit for breakfast. She has Special K with blueberries and hazelnut coffee. The whole kitchen feels roasted, warm. My mother toasts pumpernickel and rye swirl, loads them with butter. I have already eaten, but I eat again. It is that kind of morning. The kind you don't want to be left out of. The kind you want to tell about, and tell about like you were there. You are there. Four generations of women at the kitchen table. Great-Grandma tells stories of the brownstone on Charles Street, and of the West Village. She says Pop grew up (or was born) near Grant's Tomb on the West Side and that they used to picnic there. She tells it his family spoke Armenian and Assyrian. She tells it she gave birth to my Aunt Maria seven weeks early, and that my mom gave birth to my brother five weeks early. And I tell you, Araceli, to stay put. I tell you to stay cozy and stay. Stay. Keep your ears open. I want more stories, want you to hear more stories. Want to spend the whole day at her kitchen table. My grandmother and mother keep the stories awake, keep them tended and warm. My grandmother keeps photographs of my grandfather all over the house, and I know it is a constant that she misses him, but I see her keep moving, keep tending, keep on. I know nothing is certain or guaranteed. I know what it is like to be alone. I am not scared to be alone. I watch, and I watch. I learn the steps of myself too.

We are this quadrant of women, all of us traveling together—but too, all of us separate and alone. We hope our partners and the ones we love will be with us, always, but we tend to ourselves too, we tend the parts of us that will be in our gardens alone. I want my daughter to remember she has arms all around her, but I want her to know how to take a bus alone. I want her to learn how to make coffee, and feed herself. How to surround herself with bee balm and people she loves, the ones who soothe and comfort her. Want her to plant phlox and invite everyone she loves to join her around her warmed kitchen table. And always, I want her comfortable alone in a garden of things she has grown.

REVOLVE

It's the middle of your Jesus
year, almost up—gliding
towards each clang of 34
each bone slinking in part
cymbals, some bass, flat
already you are an orchestra
of a woman—playing.

Your mother, an odd 63
daughter an odd 21 months
of un-surefooted-ness,
language, un-interrupt of day.
Sure, it is pleasure, all of you
roiling in the world at once—
21, 63, 33 & your grandma
her—93, this quadruple up
coupling of numbers towards.

Decidedly, there is more
you want. A red bicycle, gold,
golden high-top sneakers, ritual
& sex, to learn Spanish, prayer
& symbols & cold tequila, shots
& oceans. An always good book,
to swim—arms, limbs akimbo
weightless in water, to breathe.

You want to be gull, bramble,
the 7 train for its un-hectic
ride through Queens & back

you want to be always riding
back to the ones you miss. You
would like to know hyacinth, phlox,
cosmos & chrysanthemum,
peony & prefer sea, waves, dunk
of water below levels & flush.

It's not enough to just turn 34.
You want a parade of dolphins,
their fins simple & gray. You think
you'd like sleep & chocolate,
ice cream & the gathering laughter
from all the lungs, exhalation
& rocked hips, antics of hands,
feet meeting sand & dust,
dirt these mouths of honey
& romp of love hung thick
& bright—around you.

KENTUCKY—YOU BE

This want travels
back roads—bourbon capital
country smell of sour mash each
dream is full of silt—this takes its time.
Simmer. Stew. Stir.

Bluegrass you are full,
full—your wide stretches & land
beneath cracked sky, preachers
& poets, verse & strand & style
& rowdy & flow. You tell it—
the stories I come back to. You
open the doors of your front
porches & kitchens & hearths
you strike the warmth & let in.

This be the place of home. Let
it be a Saturday night or some quiet
weekday hunger. Let it be
starving & poised, raucous &
demure. All things, let it holler
& moan, be the bass, be the drum,
be the peacock & the treble, be
the tremor & the starved. The savor
& the tender. The ventricle &
all the taste buds of all the tongues
awake & sweet, sweet ribs
& fingers drenched in sugar & sauce.
& all the shots down all the throats,

& all that burns.
Let it douse what yearns.

This be the spot for family—be the home
coming, be the cake-like cornbread,
be the Kentucky, the South & Hilltop
down home. Be it all. The catfish
doused in hot sauce—the brown beans, spooned
up, the ham hock & the drench of yes. To
every plate & drink/drank that reminds us of back.
Back. That reminds us what it takes
to know a place, someone, the way
we all want to be known.

Home you welcome us to your long, sturdy
table. Every time. To this hunger, this love—
love of salted breath—you quench.

BALM

for Aracelis, Carla, David & New Orleans

I am standing on skulls—mounted
vertex cradling all the weight of me,
with all my ancestors' names scratched
in & it is holy. & God is a woman
her palms facing loam & clay
four armed wholly pregnant belly,
one who is full. Is mother, fertile,
or not. Charged & open inside. Each
day is new. A chain—I am collecting
for you—them, for you. Collecting
each new way the body holds shape,
begins to multiply, is opened. Is wide.
Fans out into another wide whole.

On our walk from Quarter to Marigny,
the upside-down bathtub legs of women
appear at Gregg's Antiques. The way the sex
peeled aside—how a thing that is not,
becomes a thing that is. Rounded breasts,
waist, beginning of hip to larger hip.
Spell bind, the creature of a spell. Bound.
Who makes it for you? Who's magic for you?

MINT JULEP

I

Taste the South, go on.
Tender, tumbled, tradition
intention, task of taste
eloquent old world heir-
looming hospitality, whose
heritage is this? You
will need this drink
when you arrive.

II

Nostalgic for what?
Old South—prim, pomp,
proper, powdered & permed,
permanent, poised, playful,
crushed, jammed, tumbled,
wide-brimmed hats, My Old
Kentucky Home—full of antiques
antiquated treasures, tales
told around bow-tied
dinner parties with all
white dinner guests. Is
this the South you
think you miss? Is this
the South they are conjuring
forever?

III

Take it apart—crack the wax
and pour your own. Smoky,
spicy new world—where your home-
coming is Irish—sure, mixed
w/ Arab & Affrilachian & Filipino
do the math 'til you exist. Exist
where they told you not to. Stir
the drinks men used to—w/ new custom.
Conjure contemporary South now.
No white glove, white club,
not outdated, old-fashioned, smelling
of mothballs & stench & old money
& confederate pride. Pride
the new shuffle—shake out the old.
Label it bluegrass still. Label it
fresh—still burning, still warm.

NOTES FROM AZIZ BAZAZ

Listen. Who can, will
be able to tell, if you don't?

All the loaves, fish, gills,
tiny bones in all the oceans.
Tell how many I've caught. Been
caught. Bruised hands. Knuckles,
then drought. Fishing line then
land. Land. Grow accustomed
to something.

To live in your name. Even patience
takes time. Take time. Enjoy
every wake of morning. Figs.
A slow swim. The barrel of high
low. Tides. Any tides against you.
The healing properties of salt-
water sticky against leathered skin.
Learn to do something well.

Learn to swim. Jump waves.
Hustle. Mark water. Tread. Hold
your many breaths. All. Grow
accustomed to disaster. Chart
any course. Your own. Oh!
The body it is a live thing. Work.

And oh. The ego. The physical
want. Desire. Take those too. Stride.

Be brutal sometimes. Sometimes
I wish I had been more so.

Take your time. But hurry. Time
will do it all. And then disappear.
How I wish I had taken more of it.

Drink thick Turkish coffee and fall
in love. Whole. Process of breaking.
It is OK to break. Down.
Apart. Jealousy is tired. You
will be too if you give it more
than it will take to work. Work.
Your fingers, heart will thank you.

The drum of who
you are. Jump.
Jump. Jump.
Woman.
Jump.

RIVER. WOMAN.

I

Downriver is always long
& always flailing, finding

where our lives begin,
intersect? You, your bones

the humped slope of nose
browned skin of home.

You, sand. You, ocean.
You, bending & me.

How many nights we sleep
alone, our bodies rising—

what it means to miss you.
What it means to expand.
What it means to be birthed.
What it means to be sacred.
What it means to go home.

Place of birth, birthing
ground. Ground that is sacred.
You that is sacred.

Bones that hold together. Bind.
Bound to you. My mother.

II

Me

I am bound to you. My mother.
You stitch me from inside. Hollowed.
Your split sheath of self, your letters
the slow cursive of your language,
can't I hear your voice, always?

Her

Lock the doors. Latch the locks.
Shut the windows. Close the blinds.
Cover up. Clean your room. Do
the dishes. Wash the clothes. Behind
your ears, yourself. Clean the floor.
Scrub. Mop the remains every day
is one that you can use to erase all
the mistakes. Blemish free.
Shine the doorknobs, pine, every
crease of space. Cabinets. Don't leave
food out. Food brings mice. Mice
bring disease. You will die. You could
die. Don't die. Don't ever die. You
stitch me from inside. I am bound
to you. Can't you always hear
my voice?

KNEAD

for David

Alter trapezius, shift splenius capitis
& splenius cervicis. Make atlas of me,
topography of back as it splays open.
Trace teres minor & major, latissimus
dorsi, deltoid & spine of scapula all.
Field my body quiet. Smooth superior
& serratus & supraspinatus, crest, caress
anatomy of spine & fish-eye & memory
make calm the heft & taut of me, please.

Translation: Rub my back. The way
you always do after night has washed
from the erupt of traffic & barking
of emergency vehicles & teenagers
with their wails & the M4 as it knocks
against our front windows, bantering
& braying against the city where you love
all of me. Every last oblique & inferior
internal & external part of muscle
all the scaling heap of me, you love.

WHAT WE DO

Become slingshot shotgun six
shooter style, sly, staunch
blade in breastbone—carve
the thick, carve the plate & bound

scar the trunktimber
of sternum, slice sacrum, be
stitchslick, knit the skin back
after sectioned incision, abdomen
un-wieldy work the muscle, exhalt
the new body—baby

bruise, brute, heavy stench
sweat the sweat, watch the tendons
stretchlean, watch the biceps
pumpglow, & the clavicula
grow stems & shit, grow redrage
don't swallow one stitchstretch
syllable—watch the way we work

bourbonwhine, wailbump, birth
Razook, Gianina, Araceli, Miriam,
Patrick, Paul, birth Elinor, Bazaz,
Dawson birth the way back fleshfresh

all the tongues in all the mouths
till ululations convulsejoint
blowfuse chickenliver hot, sauce
& blood, cornmeal, gums & funk,
catfish fried salt & saints

do the dirtywork wreck, dance
blinkfish, razorsly, salmonquick
do the slide, slide, wind & whoa
& whoa. God. This
is the thing we do.

II. INHERITANCE

BODY PARTS—THEN

Pelvis: Noun
What I used to gyrate. Hip shake. Shimmy. Sex it up, both good and mediocre and real fucking good. Pelvis. See Graceland. Basin. Pelvic floor. See the "Electric Slide." Grind. See MTV and Madonna's "Like a Prayer." Pelvis. Check Left Eye—the limbo contest at Whispering Wheels—how low your hip bones can go—Forever. See: body suits, hula hoops, neon. Go on.

Abdomen: Noun
See: Green ruffled bikini. See metallic purple. See belly button ring paid for in quarters at the Radcliffe Tattoo Parlor. See suntan lotion—perfectly flat when lying beneath. Check midriff baring. Waistline. Hard-on. See crop tops and low-slung jean shorts you never wash. See. Silver hoop. Infection. Goose bumps. Bloat. Plank position.

Hips: Noun: Body Part: Below Waist
Reference Hilltop, where they sold you cases of Sterling while in your Purple and Gold Tigers cheerleading uniform. See toe-touches—how far apart your legs can go. See hands that are not yours. Latitude and leopard print. See pleather and vinyl skirts from Avalon on Bardstown Road where you are not cool—then or now. Hips. Reference Bobby Brown and his "Prerogative"—Color Me Badd's "I Wanna Sex You Up." I do. Go on, be 15 again. Don't hesitate when the dance circle widens around you—drop, bump, fist pump, hold and gel it slow. Don't think about all the ways your body will move thick without you. Hold on to it good. Grind it silly. Lick your lips. Twirl those—

HOW TO SURVIVE HIGH SCHOOL

Do the mathematics of exist, the rhythm of division—how to raise a girl to be a woman—to be you, or like you—but take away all the dumb shit you did.

Subtract acid and selling weed at an AC/DC party—minus drunk in any field, racist slurs by guys who were supposed to be your friends. They're not. Minus whippets on the Panama City beach strip—getting in the trunk of some guy's car to get into his condo to drink even more. Do not get into the trunk of anyone's car. Ever. Don't ask a priest to buy you a case of Natty Lite—he won't do it. Don't let Alex Graham, who keeps a brick of weed in the trunk of his car— always—take you behind the endless yawn of suburbs, to the pond Jessie and Laura skinny-dipped in and get you so high after play practice that the whole Bardstown, Kentucky, sky looks horrendous/glorious. Don't sneak into a city pool—ever—even if you know how to swim (and you will), and even if you somehow—against every odd—and because you cheated—are a lifeguard and could save anything and anyone from drowning. And you could because you can dive, do the breast, free, back, butterfly and you know if there was a drowning you would be there.

But don't be a hero. No one wants you dead—you can never die little girl.

Don't take a shower in the men's locker room with Justin Price, or any Justin Price–like characters. He will end up not answering your phone calls—even though he tells you your lips taste like sno-cone and chlorine and you'll like it but secretly balk at the metaphor because you two are in a fucking pool after all. Do not fall for un-original men or women. They will exhaust you. I promise.

Imagine yourself the journey, the length. Don't drink shots of tequila with Mike Johnson and Melissa on a snow day, and don't wear a hat with the worm crawling from the top of it that Mike's dad gives you all and then take pictures—they will all come back. Life is a rotation. And don't do a keg stand after all those shots because you think it will make James Pierce or some other idiot think you are sexy and cool. You will do it and then sit back on the pool table, un-cross your legs, and vomit all over the concrete basement floor.

Don't go back the next weekend for more. Mike Johnson will end up in rehab. So will Ryan (who is still there and 33), and so will Chris Mayes and so will Blake Mayes.

You will get out. It's true I got out, but sometimes I think, just barely.

WHO YOU WERE, WILD: ADJECTIVE, WILD-ER, WILD-EST

1.   Untamed, as in: not tamed or domesticated—I've not been domesticated yet—my mother who says she could have been/was/is a seasoned domestic—her calling, that and/or a nun. As in—unleashed, bare, dangerous. As in I won't be wearing your habit/cross, but will exchange for miniskirt/tube top/high black heels/cigarettes/weed/a drink, please

2.   Growing or produced without cultivation or the care of humans—meaning—un-watered, not tended, though I am no spider plant/hydrangea/honeysuckle/ugli fruit/cherry blossom/banana tree—trust me I can water myself wet enough—don't need your cultivation

3.   Uncultivated, uninhibited, or waste, as in—wasted—as in—drunk/itty drunk/tore up/as fuck/blinded/blindsided/broken/lost—uninhibited—as in—naked/riled up/funnel/dusted/toasted/dared/double dog dared/triple dog—you know the rest

4.   Uncivilized or barbarous: shouting/vomit/urinating in public/hallucinations/lying/lying to get your way/lying to punish/lying for fun/skinny-dipping/drugs you were told to avoid/positions you were told not to do until you were married/blow jobs/beheading/blatant anything

5.   Of unrestrained violence, fury, intensity, etc. Etc.—as in—show up at your house at midnight—as in—leave crazy fuck emails/phone calls/shout-outs/text messages/calls on your beeper—beep, beep, beep—blackouts/bloody fists/brazen/hollowed/lively/lunacy

6.   Watch me

RECKLESS, MEASURED

When the man hocks
his loogie, darting from mouth
to leaves, dirt all still
on the ground from September
near the tree & reckless weeds
surrounding, covering,
rather than crawl from it, you hike
your sturdy baby leg over the fence
& walk right in. Hands, fingers,
nails on both hands digging deep,
to some unknown dirty place.
Hell with it. You give me a look
like, *don't be weak, Mom.* Not afraid
of trash, discarded Sour Patch Kids,
condom wrappers, popgun remnants,
yellowed cigarette butts, balloons
losing steam, strewn across J. Hood Park.
You guffaw at cockroaches, shout
bug, hi bug, wave to the mouse wheeling
from the woodpile near Hudson River,
crown yourself in wood chips, pile
loose grass over your eyes, mouth.
Declare home with your legs buried
in rocky sand, concrete land.
On the 1 train you rest your head
against grimy window, toes kicking
into space, all glee on your face.
This is how I know
you are a New Yorker.

IT'S TRUE

after Barbara Ras

You can't have it all—but you can have your mom's hands on your back on a rainy Saturday afternoon in October and her mama's soup cooling on the stove and whole wheat panella to soak in olive oil. And your one and only daughter strolling her life-sized Elmo doll to see the alpacas and their glorious spit at the Central Park Zoo. You can have the twelve ducks huddle up the man-made stairs on the Bay—their sides swathed in patches of royal blue and red—you can have your daughter's insistent quacks, her howling for them and her unmasked glee when they flock/fly up into sky. You can have her quiet conversation with the orange and black monarch lying still on its side in the street: *Are you OK? No? Are you dying, little butterfly?* You can still have birthed a child—abdomen scarred open. You can have coffee every morning, calm, or the search for it. You can have the *New York Times* digital subscription, because isn't everything all the time digital anyway? You can have that warm sweater you come back to. You can't have everything, it's true, but you can have a new life, one full of art and New York City, full of shit and dirt and palmetto bugs that scurry beneath you. You can have prayer—even if you aren't religious—and stained glass in a Lutheran church with a garden paint by number club where you commune/become community and Mother Cabrini's canonized, enshrined body at the altar where your daughter asks questions and is religion too. You can have your own mother's Hail Mary at night when the dark is too quiet to sleep and you are too afraid to do anything—the slide of her rosary beads through fingers and all the words in all the worlds you've still got to learn—all of this, you can have too.

WORDS YOU SAY

The first time you say
Oh, Goddammit, we are in Kentucky,
your grandparents watching, their eyes
on me & my parenting skills
nil.

I don't tell them
you already say shit sometimes
when being changed
and your father who told you
Only say shit at home with us.

Or that last week, while editing
you said hi to the images
and instead of hi Mommy, hi
Dad, hi cat, hi doggy, you
said *hi fucker* to the man
on the screen & laughed hard.

You are only 18 months old
& already you've got a mouth
on you, & the world, *fuck*
I think, but don't say out loud
anymore.

Though gosh darnit & shoot
& oh dang don't suit me
or the kind of woman I am
or the kind I want you
to be.

Words little girl
I want you to know their use
when a good Goddammit
is appropriate & good, God
words like fuck & shit & hell
their place & how to use
manipulate, right them
into place right there
where language does
what it does and makes
what is right—right.

RESERVOIR

I

Watch the expansion—teeth
full of saccharin, sucrose, sugar,
metallic, concentrate, cane, full
of syrup, the sticky-ness of any-
thing sweet enough to crack
a filling.
Take a filling
watch it load w/ salt, soda—
pop, synthetic negligence
addictive additive—how you
introduce the body—how to love it,
how to feed, harness, not neglect,
abandon, let loose—un—harness.

II

Take the body—its glob & full throttle towards age-evity, flit, flirt of taut,
softening. Take the bloated bulge barnacle to feel. Take the weight, soft head of
baby, the baby weight too—take that, her arms, limbs, legs, snout & hoof of
hers inside you—water amniotic anything thinning of membrane brain & what
protects—embryotic sac flung from—molecules, the way a belly is marked—
stretched, sub-cutaneous fat—fate.

III

Whole of abdomen, not flat
smooth, stoned, not Barbie
doll, *Pin-Up*, *Hustler*, hustled
into tight tops, triangular bikinis,
not barely 21—not barely 31.

IV

Consider the Mee Rojak & Green Curry
salty fat shrimp & green peppers
rice noodles w/ peanut sauce, two
Tsingtao & Beerlao Dark beer—helping after
helping of white rice, its husk & germ
stripped, straight to the small intestine
its instant glucose & fructose
eat until full—always.

Consider then, the body that is,
& the head still
bemoaning the body
after baby, consider the expanse—love
love it

SHE HAD A FACE

for Carolyn Thomas & Connie Culp & all the
many faces of others

All I'm saying is
she had a face. Jawbone,
chin, cheekbone, two eyes,
nose curved just so, fore-
head, temple, two lips,
margin of mouth. All her
teeth, shining in their sockets.
Cavities. Crowns & all. A throat,
clavicle, nostrils, bridge, lashes,
eyelids, eyeballs, eyebrows. The whole
shebang. Hairdo, her hairline
just so. So she had it all. The skin
is an organ. Is a musical beating
pulsing thing. Prickled. Sensitive
like skin is.

Did he see all that
when he shot her?

When the bullet went
from gun to face. Bull's-eye.
Her whole identity misplaced,
missing person-ed. Concaved.
The puff & structure shattered.
All her bones dust inside.
Her old face on milk cartons,
in newspaper ads. Un-recognizable
wasn't even the word they could use.

He must have thought—*Yes.*
As if a bullet is a plan, his
rode into everything she used to be.
& so I am sure
he imagined her broken.
Gone. No one claiming her
at the morgue. No touch-
ups by undertakers, no
magic, makeup, concealer
he must have thought
he'd done her in.

Oh, you underestimate
the anger of skin.
I hear her say, her new
face still un-figured, still up
& struggling, but on, & on him
& tasting. Saliva. Smelling the trail
to him. Her teeth brand-new again,
ready for the supple of his neck.
Planning ways to un-figure
him. No bullets. How weak
can you be. She thinks. No.

I'll wrap my new mouth around
a yes. & you'll see me. Watch
my fresh face. Be born again.

NEW YORK CITY—COME ON

after Jamaica Kincaid

This is how you move to a new city—its hustle and wide streets w/ no rules and no fly shoes to get you where you need to be gotten. No friends and a limited amount of cool clothing—your hair the frizzy mess it has always been. This is how you tell the cab driver that you are lost before you even get in the backseat— your two suitcases huddled around you and no cell phone, no email to busy you/ distract you from the fact that you are alone and scared. This is how you walk the streets: William to Fulton, Fulton to Broad and the South Street Seaport then down to Battery Park. This is how you circle the edge of the city you love but do not know. This is how you spot a rat in a squirrel's clothing in Tompkins Square Park, or Union Square. Be careful. A rat can fool you—can dart across lawns at night in the dark and leave you. Like men. Like a man can fool you. This is how you date a boy—his long hair covering one eye—artful. This is how you eat copious amounts of Italian food and down cheap wine so that this is how you are always hungover. This is how you date another boy, and another, and this is how you can tell a boy from a man. This is how you cook an egg, make a strong cup of Earl Grey tea. This is how you make friends, how you catch a water bug psycho killer roach in your kitchen. This is how you come to love Zahida and Fely. This is how you down a beer. This is how to eat a fish with all its bones and teeth. This is how you roll a dosa with cashews and coconut chutney. This is how you give blood. Yours, and this is how you hear your father's voice when the towers fall and this is how you ride the trains. The 6 will take you to Brooklyn Bridge, but not further. The 4, 5 will take you from the Bronx to Brooklyn, but never to Queens, and this is how you'll know the difference. This is how you cry in a diner while eating a cheeseburger. This is how you cry on Sixth Avenue. This is how you cry to your mom on the phone, even though you swore you wouldn't do that, and this is how you ask for help, move furniture, call home, sleep in sheets covered in soot and dust. This is how you turn 23. This is the West Side

Highway. This is Tortilla Flats and the hula-hoop contest that you win. This is the hot pink hula hoop, its rocking flounder around your hips. This is Manley's, and the boy who brought you a bottle of California wine. Watch him walk away, watch you. This is his roof in Williamsburg. And his. This is you walking away. Again. This is the coat you wear. These are the boots. This is when you weep on the plane home. This is when you come back for more.

ONCOMING

I see you girls
from Queens—your international
whole girl selves. With hijabs
& black horn-rimmed glasses,
your nerdy cardigans—buttons downed
& neon lime leggings, patches of crows
on your '90s-style jean jackets—I see
you—all of you.

Love of the Beatles, Rolling Stones
natural haired, multiracial, all language
speaking selves. All of you unhinged
girl-women with all your bones, teeth,
brains & all in tact & shining,
with your flip genius humor & free
laughter on the LIRR—home
to families who protect all
of your cerebellum-heavy selves.

I see you guitar riff, relay girls,
your track star, vice president
of the Muslim Student Union selves
& nighttime obsessed readers of *Twilight*

*Edward & Bella—see Edward is the vampire. I can't believe you don't know that,
and of course Bella is just the human and of course they fall in love even though they
really can't, ya know? So, but they do and then they have a baby and there's this freaky
vampire/human inside her that tries to like claw its way out. It's really messed up and
so awesome. You should totally read it and then see the movie too.*

I see you girls
who tell me all the many,
many things I should be doing
with the short life ahead of me—
comparatively to yours, it's true.
There is much I want to say,
but listen each afternoon instead.
Imagine us all girlfriends, soccer
teammates, gossips on Friday nights,
sure, there is much you do not know.

But the tracks take us all—never mind
you girls will never fall in love w/ vampires
or werewolves & your children w/out hooves
or fangs. All of you will venture
into nights alone, sometimes afraid
& sure there will not be fairy tales,
not the ways you've been told.
But there will be gold sky on rides home
& warm food sometimes & the arms
of all those who brought you up
to be the girl-women selves
you are becoming.

MERCY

for Justice Williams—fourth-grade student at PS 33
who took her life on April 7, 2013

Because you were only nine—when they tell me—I lose all breath and clutch
palm to belly and say the names of both my daughters, even the one who has
not arrived—but has. You were just nine, just in this world 108 months. Only
thirty-six seasons saw your hair and bones grow, stretch of legs—puberty hadn't
even found you, not your period or first kiss—not even old enough for middle
school. In the photograph w/ your mother and your new baby brother, you look
happy—glasses on, all your smiling teeth in a row and no, we did not meet. I did
not teach you about line break or how to write about the muscle of your heart,
but oh, how many nine-year-old girls I have known, have seen slumbering in
their bodies. And today, I walk past PS 33 in its hulk of pillars and the 4 train
hustling above Jerome Avenue and Fordham Road w/ its gyro trucks, Mexican
groceries and Dominican coffee stands and the one diner teeming w/ hatch-
ing termites and the Barbie birthday cake in the window of the bakery w/ her
icing-ed body and candle-ed head. You will not see ten or thirteen or nineteen or
thirty-five, and will not get to see all the mercy and guts and pain this world can
make happen. I will miss the face I didn't pass this afternoon on a seventy-eight-
degree April day—where the streets were crammed w/ girls your age who will be
awake in the morning. How I wish you would be awake in the morning. How
I think of your mother carrying all the gentle weight of you down, down into
the streets—your name on her tongue—all the girl you will forever be, still—
always—carried in her arms.

HOW DO YOU HAVE SUCH A YOUNG SOUL & SUCH AN OLD FACE?

for my student Nichelle

You should wear more beautiful clothes,
Rachel, my second-grade student, tells me.

& Nichelle, my high school student,
tells me in a poem that I have an old face.

How do you have such a young soul
& such an old face?

Prompting me to stop smiling so much
un-adjusting the lines—subtle, or not

search the faint ones, forehead, drooped
underneath eyelids, the drone of neck.

I am only 30 years old. 33 now, but then
I was only 30. What 30 does—did to a face.

Nichelle wants to know how did my face
mine, the one stretched over bones, get so old?

I study its wrinkled chisel, its years in this
sun and wind and desert worn-out on me

its spread and compass, contortions
every collapse, crack-up captured on skin.

Saltwater, chlorine, 97-degree days unblocked
broken blood vessels, worried lines, acne

the inflammation of many years here
on the surface of sound, of never holding back.

Let it be old, young, young girl, let this face
exhaust you, this skilled, surfaced breakdown

go ahead ask my old face how it got there
watch it flaunt its fossiled swagger.

TAKING A PART

I

In your Jesus year, your body is soft. The core of you at least. Most of you is
jelly, rolled, shaked, and whoa-ed. This be the body you emerged with. This—
the body you take, dunk in saltwater, bay, shore. These be the legs that have toe-
touched, electric slide-ed, spread, squatted, suntanned. Be the belly that's been
sit-upped, pierced, ballooned, sick, pregnant, swole. These be the breasts licked,
plied, pulled free, bra-less, swum naked. These be the hips. This be the hair, loss
of curl, its gray now ambling in uninvited, spiraling, sprouting from scalp, un-
embarrassed. This be the vulva, still poufed and full of still black hair. These—
the muscles, the heave and struck of weight. Bend of wire, mesh, hall of throat.
Waist, ride, hide. Riding the all of you.

This be the naked body—

II

Knuckled stump of hard, of rib. Abdomen
spread wide—expanse the lotus, lower—
shell of me. I love this sapling-ed tongue
ventricle & all the ribbed shift inside
of whole, scapula & their winged prayer
across the back of me. The back, brain
& all its nerve. Design, I love
the house of my lungs, all their breath,
bramble, shards & heft. Love the clavicle
jutting, empty space. Jawbone of larvae,

heatened, sliver of limbs. I do
love you body. You husk, you words still
I haven't thought of—you this. You this. You
this. Body.

You gain four ounces, size
of a foot & growing. Ears

of corn resemble you now.
Lean still, but plumping quick.

Your lungs are branches, breath
of respiratory tree reaching.

& your cells help your air
sacs inflate. You're inflate-

able now. Puff & bump
across abdomen. Skin still thin,

translucent & I can see—
it seems right through you.

Head to heel, you are rutabaga now,
13 and a half inches & halfway over

a pound—the color of your hair
visible now & fat is sure & coming

to your frame. The wrinkles
beginning their smoothing out.

Every day you are more baby
than you were before, umbilical

cord still hanging thick between
my body & yours & hope we feel

this joined,

forever.

EXPECTING

We walk the path from your house—around the wasteland of a baseball field and beyond. Tucker pulls at his leash and rushes forward beyond us. It's 85 degrees and I long for the shade. I am too many months pregnant and you are just 20 days away from your divorce being finalized. I am out of breath, but we keep walking. Arizona's fat sky is a wide blister above us. We are 30-year friends the two of us. I am 31 and you will be 31 in June. The age feels exhausted already. You don't want to make any more big decisions for a while. I don't blame you, but want you to move back to Kentucky, and even though I don't live there anymore, I know that it's home and want you to come home. But I don't push, and I don't say that I am proud of you because that might sound condescending and asshole-like and most of all I just want you to know that we drove across California and Arizona to lay eyes on you and your home and to throw our legs up together and laugh—waste away whole days like we used to. To see the orange tree in your backyard and smell the jasmine and orange blossom, to watch the wide expanse of desert sprawl out—see the mountains and peaks of things. To walk your dog with you and see Tempe in the morning, to sit outside with you in another state, another time with you and your sister and David and eat shrimp tacos, guacamole, tamales, and David's 20-buck burrito. Get it all in. To visit your school and adoring high schoolers with their funks and nerdy quips and your home that is warm and on flat land and most of all to say a silent *fuck you fuck you fuck you* to the man who did what he did to you. Eat at your favorite Italian mom and pop shop in a strip mall because no joke everything in Phoenix/ Tempe/Scottsdale is in a strip mall, but still—it's good, and good to see you and good to see you doing well too. There is much in this life that takes time and much of it we have still to go. I want, friend—to travel with you through all of it.

Networks of nerves abound. Baby center
says—this week your ears are better than

before. Sensitive too. Sound, as it gets
to you—pronounced & patterned. Too,

outer, inner, middle ear & eustachian tube
form—tiniest of drums & canals open—

you are auditory now little girl. All ears
as they say. We no longer need whisper

since your malleus & incus are brand-new
& ripe for the hearing. Say your name

even louder. From our mouths love,
love—through your lobe to your labyrinth.

Love.

Though 13 is supposed to be unlucky it's good
to know there are only 13 left on decline.

Because at just 2 pounds your father calls you
both Wu-Tang & Shaolin—the way you move oh

is already up & intense & fly. You are no cauli-
flower, no. You are all dragon & firework, all

bird of paradise, tightrope walker & sleuth
below skin. Rhythmic rhythms bound inside

from you to the inside of me. Bumping religion.

III. CONCEPTION/CONCEPT

THINGS YOU ARE

You are a nest you are bird's eggs you are incubating you are a beak
 travelogue mountain crest cliff girl.
You are eleven stars seaside elevation elevated you are lucid still dreaming nest of
girl girlhood nestled close twigs & branches of things you are orchard girl orchid
peony blossom crooked & skull you are escape & relocation small as stone com-
ing soon you.
 Premier girl
always arriving you are physical confession a dragon flying you are wings surely
sky heat lightning you are guitar-ed riffs every country hill I've ever gotten high
on traveled my journals open religion swimming in rivers ocean waves a jellyfish
fish gill girl of fins & things you are a tail the trail I take home.
 You are home
the shape of blue seashells eggshells bath water & ships sails sailed boats
docks oyster shells you are peeking out collected limbs you are peach trees
 & fall
 falling.

WATER SIGN

Already a lullaby inside.
Your palms to belly, breath
on hip. You are changing,
beginning. Too. & you,
baby girl, or boy. Or two.
Are just gills. Still. Heart in
mouth. Red burst of newness.
Fins. Fish or fowl. Shrimp
are larger than you.

Still, you are breaking me
apart. Him too. Our hearts
& lungs & gills. Bursting
you are stretching all,
all of us. Open.

UPRIVER IS SPIRIT

One more—for David

And you are. Upriver. Spirit. Fly,
the flyest of things that don't split open.
You are beer in church pews, slow
the grind you do inside. Wicked too.
Your shoulder in teeth,
gripped bite of ear on tongue.
Your body rooted against mine
the expanse of legs, willed.
Time, all time, all the time
all the time for you. You
are jasmine sun
shine. Liquor. Warm sheets
11 P.M. anywhere. On the cusp
not splitting open. Manning up
is you manning up—loving that term.
Is being cooked for—sometimes cooking,
but eating rice and beans at Mother's.
In New Orleans with you. Upriver.
Oh, you are.
Mailboxes, fresh, cool stamps.
Letters. Yours. The long car rides.
Being in a place with history. You
making me a history. Our house.
The way you make me a house,
way you tend me, your love for me.
Your raucous second line desire for me,
the every idea of desire.

Who gets to ask for it. The way you
ask me for it.
Ramble, ramble of the way you do.
You do. You do.

BEFORE YOUR ARRIVAL

The ones who brought your father here, come. Bring
with them whole almonds, dried berries & clementines
wrapped in cloth. Their clothes & smart shoes too.

They come looking for the place I've taken your father.
Looking for the New York City that could rival home.
Your Abba loves the East Village, its graffiti, trash
& all the languages on all the streets. On 1st Avenue
between 12th & 13th we visit the Philippines. Elvie's Turo Turo.

But this trip, he wants to see more. So,
we travel to Little Philippines, Queens, 69th
off the 7 train, off the 7 the whole of Queens
opens wide for us. Travel agents & whole-
sale, send anything back for cheap, travel
for cheap, return, return. We buy OK
magazines by the handful for gossip
Tagalog with English subtitles, glossy
photos, Pacquiáo, his chiseled grin everywhere.

And we eat. Krystal's where they serve
marinated pork belly, sinigang na baboy,
kare-kare, pancit bihon & lumpiang sariwa,
I listen close to it all. Deep-fried ruffle fat,
poolee noodles with shrimp, milkfish.
Your Abba fake orders pork blood stew
but I am sure I would eat anything here
because this is how much I trust the two
who brought your father up in the world.

We eat sing-sing & pork in tamarind soup.
This is how to say snack in Tagalog: *merienda*,
Merienda is snack. This is how to say ice cream
in Tagalog: *halo-halo, halo-halo*
is ice cream. This is how to leave your country.
Don't look back. You will only see the islands
melting away. Halo-halo. This is how to feel
of one place & of one more.

Back home, we sit, get caught up. I read
about mansions in Manila, how to make millions,
face-lifts & silken hair, red lips, muscles & beauty.
In Tagalog, I muddle through, while your Abba
laughs, translates, translations get muddled too.
This is how to raise a baby in two places at once, & how
it feels to live and move in two worlds. At once.

FINAL INSPECTION

Oh body. In your husk. Shelled and sweeped beneath—the sex, the G-spot conversion.

Kegel and prep, perineum. Pulse, pulse. Prepare the limbs. Their lawless stretch. The pelvis and its Elvis tilt, massaged below. Prep the canals, all of them. The hip, femur, the loose-ed, floating bones. Beneath all that sheet of skin. The crank of tailbone, its steady below, begin of spine. Supple-indent of flesh, fine.

Body, do your thing. That muscled dip. Tendon to intestine to blood, cell, to hinge and bend of waist too. Oh body, how the tailbone spins open. Ache at every turn around. Breasts with your all.

The clamp of small child flail & dismantle—dismount. Come body. Come on, baby.

TAKE TWO

You are so many things Celi. An automobile. Train. Coop. Phone calls coming in. Celery root. Radish. Cabbage. Sea foam. Underwater. Bridge. Boat. Land. The connect between. Between. Heat lightning. Soul. Records and soda. Salty pretzels. Peanut butter. Jelly on biscuits. Buttermilk. A hot oven. A rocking chair in July. Summer. A wave coming in. Going out. The beak of a bird. Seagulls. The cry of gulls in the morning. A calm bay. Before a storm. You could be a storm. Heat lightning. Lemons on trees. An avocado. A ladder leaned on a fruit tree in August. A guitar. Trombone. A funny saxophone girl. You are a crest. One half of the moon. Syntax. A xylophone. Slow dance. Hip shuffle. Shuffle board. A lazy cruise. Riverbed.

Creek bed. Sifted mud. Mud bug. A New Orleans Saturday night. Soul Rebels. Lost bread and bourbon over ice. Ice cream sundaes. A car ride. Highways in Kentucky. Up north. Espresso shots with lemon rind. Peels of things. Masks and Mardi Gras beads. Awake at 4 A.M. Krystal burgers. Beef. Tacos. Fiesta. Plane rides into distances. Getting sleepy. Sleep deprived. What we want. Need. You be.

BIRTH

If it hadn't been full-on August, and then turned so abruptly into September, and if the baby had been the only thing on your mind, and you had taken the customary tour of Beth Israel Hospital on 17th Street and 1st Avenue, you would have declined their services. You would have seen the torn through, discarded magazines from 2009 with their overdone, outdated celebrities, and their out of style frocks and hairdos. You would have seen stained armchairs, everything old, the bathroom's broken tiles, yellowed posters of cats and babies. It was not the place you imagined giving birth. Not the gleaming, glisten of some super fly, sleek waiting room and fashion from 2010. It was not up-to-date. Nothing was up-to-date. And this was New York City. Your birth was supposed to be glamorous, with shiny accoutrements, and a glistening shower with high-end toiletries. *What happened*, you think, as you make your way into your flimsy gown.

In the hospital, waiting to be sliced opened and halved, David photographs you, your raspberry lip balm, mascara, silver hoop earrings, your wide smile and the containers of Avant Gauze that you both get a kick out of. *So punk rock*, you think, and are glad you live in this place. You look glowing still, alive, awake. Having given in to this—city, grit and your mother saying—*you're the one who wanted to live, fall in love, give birth in that godforsaken city*. So *fuck it* you think. Might as well be bejeweled when they lift your daughter from you.

And you are. And they do. In the surgery room the doors close making everything cold, sterile, but David is in scrubs beside you, holding you. And the doctors—the ones you adore—talk about the chilly weather and you close your eyes, body numb from your ribs down until you hear the girl who could not be anyone else's girl but yours. And you are not upset that they clean and wrap her body before handing her to her father. Then to you. Because when she sees you and your wet eyes and cheeks too, she licks the salt right from your face. And you know you could not ever be any other place than this one.

Fetal position—think birth—think primary colors
the primary. Primal of it all.

You pulled, taut jawed, hairbone. Clavicle, your
far toed foot dangling into the thin, cleaned air.

Your wings fire made, spell of you. Way your arms
span. Spin out from your delirious body.

Body crouched—is a palette, is a bank of things
the clanging of a pinball machine—not

broken, not slate, not ashen, or ash
not made of dust. Internal color—struggled out

what it takes. Where the body might, could
live, where the muscle could tear, fold, be un—

loosened. Where the tendon, hamstring
achilles, where the heel could sprain, stretch

along the places where the body can. Where it
do. Reside and bend. Come on.

The body it does come back. Come
on. Come on.

This is where you birthed a girl. And don't ever not call it birth. You did. You
were there. All of you. You birthed her. You did. This is the corridor you walked
down at Beth Israel Hospital on the corner of 17th and 1st, after a C-section—
no wheelchair and your mother- and father-in-law helping you down the ramp.
This is your husband hailing a cab and your suspension of disbelief and your
swollen, swollen breasts and your *fuck you* to the woman from the Upper Breast
Side who assured you your new bra would fit. *Fuck you.* This is the street you
came home to: corner of Fort Washington and 177th. The place you brought

your four-day-old daughter home in a yellow hybrid taxi cab. This is you in disbelief that you have a child, and she is yours. Because you are unsure of every-thing, and now, now that she is here you are sure you need to know more than you do. All you want—ever—is to protect her and build a net, buoy around her and scavenge the world, Internet, the streets for her. Dodge the shit on the street, and God, there is so much shit on the street, and protect her from everything, people, herself, all the damage she could inflict.

All you know is that she is everything, and that everything scares the shit out of you. And too, the world, you think, seems to be falling apart and you are trying to hold on—but—you found a water bug in her bedroom this morning and you are not sure if you and New York are even in love anymore and you feel sometimes like nothing is enough and you feel unkempt, and your clothes (all of them) are bad, and your haircut is like Jane Fonda's, and Jane Fonda is not the young starlet you were hoping you would resemble. And you are 33. And the year is 2012. You watch the news in the middle of every night. In Israel and Iran, they prepare bomb shelters and gas masks. In Wyoming, on an Indian reserva-tion the size of Delaware and Rhode Island combined a girl, 14, is dragged dead by her brother and cousin. And I am thinking of ways to protect you, and I am thinking of ways to protect all the girls who are not my daughters. I am thinking of them too.

Because you were pulled from me.
Because I love a scar that lasts.
Because I did not use shea butter or Vaseline.
Because I understand what it is to be cut-incision-ed & bloody
someone else's hands inside abdomen
abdomen cut open, muscles sliced.
Because I was numb from the ribs down.
Because you have a set of ribs too & already
such lungs, lungs little one.
Because I have nursed you from breasts.
Because you have breasts and will bleed
someday. Hymen broken. You have a hymen
the tissue of a thing. Bladder & gall.

The force of you pulled out.
Because you licked my face. Puppy. Cub.
Fish, little lobster clawed & twine.

Because to have a daughter
is to always feel sliced in two.

HOLIDAY

It's Christmas Eve, 2010. We have what feels like the newest baby on the planet. She is ours and she is new. She has been in the world just two months and everything feels exhilarating and nauseating and brilliant and horrific—all at the same time—or all within a 24-hour time period, depending on how much: sleep, coffee, Percocet, beer, bourbon, reality TV, icing, cream cheese, Velveeta, or leftover stuffing from Thanksgiving that I have plied myself with. It's touch-and-go for the most part, and you're either laughing hysterically, or crying hysterically—either way you are mostly hysterical.

It is Christmas Eve. We are in Kentucky, the Bluegrass, our home, and although we have lived in New York for nearly twelve years, Kentucky still/always feels like home.

He drives me out to a lonely (maybe the loneliest) Waffle House in all of Kentuckiana. The booths are red vinyl and there's a Willie Nelson album on the jukebox. An older couple is eating breakfast in the corner, and two young men sit at the counter. We sit close enough to the grill that we can see it sizzle and blow grease into the air. Our waiter might be the slowest waiter in the history of all Waffle Houses. Most times I wouldn't care, but tonight I have my two-month-old daughter on my mind: did she eat enough, did she poop, did she cry when her grandma put her to sleep, does she miss me immensely, does she think we've abandoned her, will she be there when we return, what if we never return . . . until I snap to attention—it's like that these days. I am in a constant state of paranoia and pure bliss. It's disgusting. Also, I'm still totally full of baby bloat (or just full of chocolate ice cream, Brooklyn Lager, oatmeal cookies, mashed potatoes and gravy bloat—whatever). None of that stops me from wanting hash browns more than anything, more even than wondering if our daughter will forget our faces when/if we return. We order: egg and cheese on toasted white bread for me, and bacon and egg for David, hash browns scattered, covered and smothered (which sounds like some dirty sex game), and a pecan waffle, which our—slow as the earth's rotation—waiter burns on his first attempt and then tells us. He is earnest. The wait feels extraordinary and the coffee burned and causing anxiety, but I breathe.

I wonder if this is what it means to leave the one thing you can't ever love enough—is this what it means to know hunger and satiation, to know want and travel and a whole life without the new one you've helped bring into the world? We eat in silence, our legs touching below the stick of the table, knowing how wide this place is—how separate it can feel and lonely. We drive fast home and hold the smallest piece of it while we can.

AWAITING THE STORM

I. What I Long For

Quiet, empty, no noise
absent chatter, sirens gone silent, no
emergency vehicles, trauma
no 4 trains screeching in-
to stations—slow bump of A
below the hearth of bed we share, no
no heaving slump of M4 ambling
to duck the curb, clumsy, outside
every window alive & humming.
Wouldn't you wheels & conductors
& brakes & whelps go still?

II. What We Make

Pots of soup. Large ones
w/ carrots & celery & onions
spinach & cannellini beans
in their soft translucent coats.
Leftover spinach dip & ziti
w/ frozen too salty meatballs.
Banana & blueberry smoothies
& bread from bakeries in Jersey
made of wheat & whole, crackers
shaped into butterflies we fly
into Celi's awaiting mouth. This
is nourishment.

III. What We Do

Appreciate: morning hours,
loss even. Early, what it is
to wake in darkness w/ your whole
body & that of your daughter—
pulse of dawn
too strong coffee
harvest—cloves—cinnamon
ice cold water & ice.

Be grateful for: power
no flooding, luck, a wash
of things, oh!
Your crying child because—
you know she is alive, breathing
has lungs and breath. Exhalation & all.

IV. What to Protect

Stock up. Fridge. Water.
What precautions to take—there
are many. Higher ground is blessing,
is a bridge, dry. Suggest: warm clothes,
anything that comforts. Extra
strong coffee & leftover dinner party pie.
Stocked everything. Take stock.
Guinness. Bottles of Syrah,
sauvignon blanc & one brick of Brie
you forgot to serve. Salsa & extra sharp
cheddar that Celi piles on. Hunger
is a thing that never disappears. Is
a thing that stays. Protect the girl.
Remember the other girl/boy children
you cannot.

HURRICANE, OCTOBER 31, 2012

That this week is a gift.
That a chicken suit, its rumpled,
poufed plumage & bellowing
orange beak during tropical
cyclone un-seasonable merge
of system to system—systemic
of oh, everything gone awry—
is a gift, sure.

Your smallest daughter dressed
as fowl in full feathers & stuffed
w/ guise & miniature Milk Duds
& dress your own cupcakes full
of sugar & sprinkles—is sweet,
maybe the sweetest part of this
flooded surge, outage of power.

That a hurricane brings the sea
& sand in place of gravel, roller
coasters rising from saltwater
with their dips & nausea like light
towers un-manned & fragile
in all their hulking glory. Amiss
amongst the baby claws of crabs
& pastel seashells that burrow
quick & steady into low tide.
& all the feet-less flip-flops
& photos of summers spent
w/ tanned legs on bungalow
front steps & Italian ice, cherry

in its liquid syrup drip. Grandma
& Pop w/ his fishing pole lilt
of 5 A.M. bringing fish to fling
back into their breath of gills.
That a hurricane knocks it all
jagged, so your memory of place
is a wandering wash.

So you bask in what you can.
The *cock-a-doodle-doo* & *bwack*,
bwack as your poultry banters
w/ the girlish devil neighbor
& the green dragon from up-
stairs & his snow princess
from 4B. Watch her peck
& waddle towards you, mouth
full of powdered bliss. Make this
this one picture. Hope the water
doesn't strip it away.

PUBERTY

Walking down 170th Street in the Bronx, I see a boy in a wolf's mask riding his bicycle. Into eternity. Into the October sun, setting behind the courthouse and Kennedy Fried Chicken and Middle School 218 where the halls smell like puberty. Into a wreck. Into the orbit of Pluto. Into adulthood. Or not. No eyes. Fur. The ripple of his 14-year-old frame. Riding. Riding.

Or maybe. It is a wolf in a 14-year-old boy's clothing. Wolf in the boogie down. Wolf rushing to catch the crowded sweat of the Bx11. Wolf on the way to in love, on the way home for dinner, roast chicken and tostones, on the way to Little Red Riding Hood's crib, or his girl's, or his auntie's, to the bodega. Wolf smoking a menthol cigarette, having a first kiss, getting to 2nd base, eating mini Snickers bars till he throws up. Wolf on a ten-speed, a BMX trick bike, turning tricks on the Grand Concourse. Wolf dressing up like Hector. Jonathan. Kaury. Dontarius. Malek. Wolf trying to get to the other side.

Or better. Wolf studying algebra, the Civil War, the scientific equation for poverty, brainstorming the effects of children and Halloween, what it means to not want to be yourself. Or easier. Wolf learning to hunt an owl, stray cat, his heart. Get it back in his chest. Wolf in the eighth grade, writing poems about lonely nights. Wolf talking trash, fighting with other, taller, more muscular wolves, with straighter teeth, and deeper voices, and more girls and more stories after school, and more goals, and more jump shots. Wolf practicing his dance moves in his bathroom mirror. Wolf masturbating endlessly. Wolf hoping his mother never, never, never enters the bathroom. Wolf being an asshole, something 14-year-old boys are prone to being. Wolf reading *Dragon Booster* comic books. Wolf lifting ten-pound weights and telling his friends they are 25. Wolf wishing he was 25. Wolf acing algebra. Figuring out how to hang on. Hanging on.

Or maybe it is just a boy in a wolf's mask riding home.

BECAUSE,

to be vomited on is to be a mother. Is to hold both your palms into a cup and catch all. Is to have the instinct to wrap arms and chest to back, salvage satin blanket, lift stuffed ninja from Tita Lisa and drag your pump bag through the rocks outside your hotel. Is to carry your 18-month-old girl through the lobby with her shivering and short breaths towards your own mother who you know will make this better. And worse, you miss the woman who cleaned all of you, always. And you want sometimes to be that girl again. Because there is a gulf of ache to know you aren't any longer and the always ache to know you are her now.

MODUS OPERANDI, OR GOOGLE SEARCH: CAESAREAN SECTION

Spin it loose. Procedure—incision, surgical
laparotomy—uterus (hysterotomy) hysteria
who said I was. Hysterical? Lower
uterine—incision. Abdomen—then uterus—
what—this process of slicing me
in two. Draped & sterilized. This
be the way you enter.

Initial incision. Multiple layers
to get to you. What it takes
to dissect one body in search of another.

Amniotic fluid. All the things
I did not learn/search/find—blind
to it all.

Disengaging baby from pelvis.
This is what it means to split into you.

THE HUNT

Look this is your daughter. Her bellowing laugh
the wild raucous of her smile & clap.

Every finger on both hands small still, 12 teeth
all of them new. Her gums still tender. Dimples

on each side. She is a whole body of a girl
who knows what she wants. & what she wants

is the Easter Bunny. *Easter Bunny where are you?*
Her chase & wail. *Walk, Mommy, walk*

her demands in a near frenzied calling, she bucks
in your arms, her squirm & wave, calls to him.

A 6′1″ man dressed as a rabbit with a yellow vest
wearing Nike Air beneath padded furry footsies.

He hop, hops toward her—his bulbous mask supporting
the wild flapping of pink ears, his soft padded middle.

Hers is already an obsession. *Easter Bunny?*
When he is out of sight she is distraught. Searching.

Searching. *Where are you?* The begging plead
he ambles, face disproportionally larger than body.

Smiling, always smiling. Your daughter is entranced.
You are horrified. But stay smiling too.

Below the Heather Garden you attempt hand holding
anything to keep her safe. Away. She smiles, shrugs you off.

Already she is a girl with a whole body. All of it hers
to flock towards what & who she chooses. Without you.

& there is nothing natural about it. City Mini
& UPPAbaby strollers compete in acrobatics
across the Mammal Halls from capuchin monkeys
to short-tailed weasels in fake wooded areas. Wipe
snot & drool from sleeping maws of toddlers dazing
towards wolverines in natural habitats, dioramas
depicting water holes teeming w/ wildlife—this
I think is enough wildlife for me. & though
the Beisa oryx & olive baboon are fascinating
it is not nearly enough to keep me from losing
my shit.

& Celi is not unique. She is wailing too, careening
from mountain lions of the canyons to 1800s bison
ambling along the prairie. Praying is what I am doing
as sweat engulfs me & I rush toward Yosemite Valley.

It's here that I wish I could become coyote. No,
not as hunter of small prey on the Great Plains, no
my wish is that I could be stuffed into the 1950s, frozen
in a yippie howl, head tossed toward the east, enough
fake water & foliage & California skies to soothe—
some planted world on the range, where yuppie,
plastic parents exist only outside the realm
of where I plant my four limbs in dirt & earth.

Mom—the spell is broken. & I am pulled dummy-
like towards the dank halls to nightingales & spotted
flycatchers, jackdaws & blackcaps w/ their silk chests

high & proud in painted sky. It is enough to wish
I was their wings & still hold my daughter
& her real hand in my paw.

FOOT OR FIST

for Miriam Elinor

Your uterus is high
Dr. Su exclaims, eyes

thrill. She steadies
Doppler to belly.

Ah, an active one.
What an alive girl,

already caffeinated
berserk jumping sliver

of skin. Death defy
dauntless—mangos

are your size & yet
arms as pulleys, thighs

& hips as somersaults,
calisthenics of buttocks

& tumble of nerve cells
inside new brain catapult-

ing from pelvis to breast
bone, placenta as trampoline.

One-pound gymnast. Dare-
devil. We've not even met,

but it's true—already
we know each other well.

HOLY, HOLY

for your entrance into the world

The expanse of hips before.
Before, smooth, landscape.

Before, belly button ringed
wild & crop topped.

The valley of 13-year-old boy.
Hands anywhere near below.

All had to traverse the space
you arrived through—from.

Pulled like trout, salmon
wild rivered fish, slick bodied.

You, brung up, heaved, lift
offed from the gulley of me.

Oh body, body with your
frisk & flock of arms, lungs.

Oh the canal of me closed
but fingers, valves, aorta flung.

Mouth, tongue, the buds of teeth,
vulva & ventricles of brain.

Matter. All of you tilted
from the hemisphere of me.